COAL, GAS and OIL
Sally Morgan

WAYLAND

First published in 2007
by Wayland
Reprinted 2007

Copyright © Wayland 2007

Wayland
338 Euston Road
London NW1 3BH

Wayland Australia
Level 17/207 Kent Street
Sydney NSW 2000

Series Editor: Jennifer Schofield
Editor: Debbie Foy
Consultant: Rob Bowden
Designer: Jane Hawkins
Cover Designer: Paul Cherrill
Picture Researcher: Diana Morris
Illustrator: Ian Thompson
Indexer: Sue Lightfoot

Picture Acknowledgments:
Jean Pierre Amet/Sygma/Corbis: 20. Remi Benali/Corbis: 15.
Jon Bower/Ecoscene: 9. Andrew Brown/Ecoscene: 25.
EASI-Images: front cover br, 7, 36, 39,45. Richard Folwell/SPL:
front cover, 17. Chinch Gryniewicz/Ecoscene: 34. HIP/Topfoto: 4.
Peter Hulme/Ecoscene: 1, 12. Alexandra Elliott Jones/Ecoscene: 27.
Chris Knapton/Ecoscene: 18. Reuters/Corbis: 40. Erik Schaffer/
Ecoscene: 22. Keren Su/Corbis: 30. Peter Turnley/Corbis: 43.
Visual & Written/Ecoscene: 33. Jim Winkley/Ecoscene: 10.
David Wootton/Ecoscene: 28.

Every attempt has been made to clear copyright. Should there be any
inadvertent omission please apply to the publisher for rectification.
CIP data
Coal, gas and oil. - (Energy debate)
1. Fossil fuels - Juvenile literature
I. Title
333.7'932

ISBN 978 0 7502 5022 1

Printed in China

Wayland is a division of Hachette Children's Books, an Hachette Livre UK Company

Contents

CHAPTER 1 Coal, gas and oil and the energy debate

The 21st century world is hungry for energy. Vast quantities of electricity are generated to power industry and homes, while billions of litres of oil are used for transportation.

21st century energy needs

The modern western home is filled with a range of electrical equipment such as televisions, DVD players, computers and kitchen appliances. There are lights in all the rooms and a supply of hot water for heating and washing. These all use energy.

The world's population is around 6.5 billion and it is increasing rapidly, especially in less economically developed countries (LEDCs). As the number of people increases, the use of energy increases, too. A person living in an LEDC uses far less energy than somebody living in Europe or North America. For example, someone in the United States uses as much as 30 times

▽ Chimneys pumping out clouds of dark, air-polluting smoke were a common sight in the industrial areas of Victorian Britain.

more fossil fuel energy than someone who lives in an LEDC such as Ethiopia or Tanzania. However, as standards of living improve in many LEDCs, more people have the means to buy goods such as refrigerators, televisions, computers and cars. The economies of large countries such as India and China are growing rapidly, and this is increasing the demand for electricity and oil.

Burning fossil fuels

The main sources of energy in the world are fossil fuels – coal, gas and oil. However, the use of these fuels causes massive environmental problems. When fossil fuels are burnt they release several gases. One such gas is carbon dioxide (CO_2). CO_2 is one of the gases in the atmosphere that is responsible for global warming.

$\triangledown$ This pie chart shows the energy sources used in 2005 to generate the world's electricity supply.

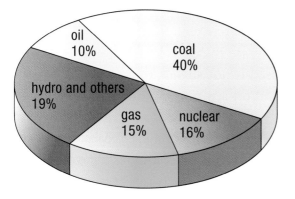

> We have to economise, be more efficient and move away from fossil fuels. Renewable energy sources such as wind, wave and solar have a role to play, but will not really come into their own until we have a way of storing their energy.
>
> Lord Ronald Oxburgh, former chairman, Royal Dutch Shell

Global warming is causing the average temperature of the Earth's atmosphere to rise. Other gases produced by burning fossil fuels include sulphur dioxide and nitrogen oxides, which cause acid rain. Acid rain is rain water with a pH value lower than 5.6. Normally, water has a neutral pH. The acidity of this rain water comes from sulphur dioxide and nitrogen oxides that dissolve in water in the air to form sulphuric and nitric acids.

Most of the world's leaders recognise that the problem of global warming has to be tackled by the reduction of CO_2 emissions. So, now we are faced with finding ways of reducing our dependency on fuels that emit CO_2 and also ways of supplying our energy needs without creating more CO_2.

Major source of energy

Fossil fuels are given this name because they have formed over millions of years from the decaying remains of plants and animals. Currently, fossil fuels are the world's main source of energy, especially in more economically developed countries (MEDCs). Fossil fuels are used by power stations to generate electricity. They power the engines of cars and aeroplanes. Substantial quantities of oil are also used in farming and industry. Oil is used to power tractors, harvesters and other agricultural equipment, and in the manufacturing of agrochemicals, such as nitrogen fertilizers.

Ancient fuels

For several thousand years, people used renewable energy sources, such as the Sun, biomass (wood, leaves, and dung), water and wind power. Sailing ships and windmills were built to harness wind energy, while energy from water was used to drive water mills. Wood and dung were burnt to provide heat and water. Solar energy has been used for thousands of years for drying crops and heating water and buildings. However, by the late 16th century many of the forests in European countries such as England, had been felled and the supply of wood was severely depleted. An alternative source of energy was needed – and that was coal.

Industrial Revolution

Although coal had been used in parts of the world for hundreds of years, it was not until the 18th century that inventors found new ways of using coal as a source of energy. This time of invention started an important period in history known as the Industrial Revolution, which lasted over the next 200 years or so.

During the Industrial Revolution, coal was burnt to generate steam, which was used to power machines such as the steam engine. Steam engines powered the first factories, steamboats and locomotives. Consequently, the use of coal to generate steam increased greatly. The next step forward was the invention of the internal combustion engine and the car, which used oil instead of coal.

Since then, the use of coal, oil and gas has steadily increased. However, this has created a problem because people are using fossil fuels at a rate many times faster than the rate at which they were formed. As a result, the rate that fossil fuels are being used is not sustainable and coal, gas and oil are running out.

▷ The vast majority of the global oil supply is used to fuel the ever-increasing number of vehicles that create congestion and pollution on city streets all over the world.

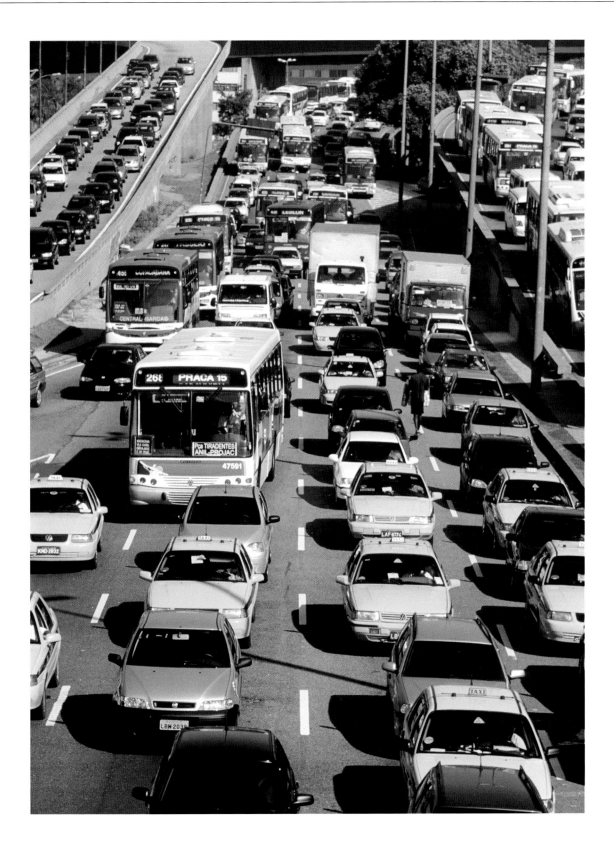

CHAPTER 2 What are fossil fuels?

Fossil fuels are formed from the remains of plants and animals that died up to 500 million years ago. Their remains were slowly buried under layers of mud and silt, called sediment, and then compressed by the weight of this sediment. Over millions of years, the compression turned the decaying plants and animals into coal, natural gas and oil. Other fossil fuels include peat and oil shale, which is a type of rock rich in carbon.

Carbon-rich fuels

Fossil fuels contain the element carbon. Carbon-rich fuels are useful because they burn in air and release a lot of energy. When they burn, the carbon reacts with oxygen in the air to form CO_2 and water. However fossil fuels release other gases such as sulphur dioxide, nitrogen oxides, carbon monoxide and soot, which pollute the environment.

Coal

A hard, brown or black substance, coal provides much of the energy used to generate electricity. It burns with a yellow flame leaving ash behind. Different types of coal release differing amounts of energy when burnt. Coal cannot be used in vehicles but it can be converted into gases or liquid fuels.

Oil

Oil is a thick liquid that is usually black, but it can be dark green or almost clear. It is made up of many different substances which have to be separated into fractions at an oil refinery (see page 16). The most sought-after fractions are petrol, diesel and kerosene. Much of the world's oil production is used in the engines of various types of vehicles such as cars, trains, boats and aeroplanes.

> " Our children and grandchildren are going to be mad at us for burning all this oil. It took the Earth 500 million years to create the stuff we're burning in 200 years. Renewable energy sources are where we need to be headed. "
>
> Jack Edwards, professor of geology, University of Colorado, US

Natural gas

Natural gas is made up mostly of methane and is highly flammable. It will cause explosions if sufficient quantities escape and are ignited. Natural gas has no odour so before it is sent to the pipelines and storage tanks, a chemical is added to give the gas a strong artificial smell. The chemical makes the gas smell like rotten eggs which means leaks can be detected more easily.

Natural gas is used mostly for heating and cooking purposes in domestic households and for powering industrial production, especially in manufacturing. Other consumers of gas include glass manufacture, metal refining, and the manufacture of wood and petroleum products.

▽ Coal briquettes for sale on the streets of Beijing, China, where coal is a readily available source of fuel for use in domestic stoves.

Natural gas is a clean-burning fuel, which means that it produces less air pollution than either coal or oil, and can be piped to where it is needed.

The effects of CO_2

A side effect of burning fossil fuels is the release of CO_2. This gas is described as a 'greenhouse' gas because it traps heat in the atmosphere, just like a greenhouse in the garden traps heat from the Sun. As more fossil fuels are burnt, more CO_2 is released. The increased levels of CO_2 trap the heat that is released, causing the average temperature of the Earth's troposphere (the lowest part of the atmosphere) to rise. Global warming is now considered a major cause of climate change.

Coal formation

Most of the Earth's coal deposits were formed about 300 million years ago. This period in ancient history was known as the Carboniferous Period, because carbon is the basic element found in coal and the other fossil fuels formed at this time.

During this period, the planet's climate was very different as it was much warmer and more humid. There were huge swamp forests with coniferous trees and tree ferns. The seas and lakes were filled with green algae.

Usually, when trees and other plants die, their remains fall to the ground and are broken down by simple micro-organisms called decomposers.

△ Most coal-fired power stations are linked to railway networks so that quantities of coal can be transported by rail from mines.

However, this did not happen in the swamp forests. When the trees died, they fell into the mud and were buried. There was no oxygen in the mud so the micro-organisms could not break down the tree remains. Instead, thick layers of dead plant matter built up in the mud.

Constant pressure

In time, a thick layer of mud or sediment buried the plant remains. The weight of the sediment pushed down on the remains, compressing or squashing them. Water was squeezed out of the remains and layers of a spongy material called peat were formed. Over millions of years, the continual pressure squeezed out even more water and the original layer of peat was squeezed to just one fifth of its original thickness. The peat had been changed into brown coal (lignite).

Over many more years, the brown coal slowly converted into a type of black coal called bituminous coal. More pressure and heat from the Earth turned bituminous coal into anthracite. Anthracite is a top quality coal that is dense, hard, black and shiny. It has a high concentration of carbon, which gives it a higher energy content than bituminous coal.

Coal is found in layers, which are called seams. A single coal seam can be many metres thick. Some seams lie close to the surface or are even visible from above ground, while others lie deep underground. Sometimes there are several seams, one above another.

Where is coal found?

Coal is found in around 50 countries in the world. More than 4 billion tonnes of coal were produced in 2004, a 38 per cent increase over the previous 20 years. Production of coal has grown fastest in Asia, while it has declined in Europe. The major coal producers are China, United States, Australia, India and South Africa.

CASE STUDY:
Coal on the Rhine

Germany is the largest coal producer in the European Union (EU) and the seventh largest in the world. Germany's recoverable reserves represent about 0.7 per cent of global reserves. The main coalfields are located close to the River Rhine and around Leipzig in the east, but much of the coal is lignite, a poor quality brown coal. Germany's rich coalfields together with large deposits of iron ore fuelled industrial growth in the late

19th century, especially in the Ruhr. The Rhine provided cheap transport, encouraging exports and industrial growth. Today, 75 per cent of coal production is used in generating electricity. Coal production has fallen since the early 1990s from over 300 million tonnes to about 230 million tonnes in 2003. This has been due to changes to the coal industry following the unification of West and East Germany, and also due to a switch to natural gas.

Coalmining

Hundreds of years ago, coal was dug from cliff faces or shallow trenches. As the demand for coal grew, people dug tunnels into hillsides following the coal seam. These tunnels were called drift mines. Once the Industrial Revolution was underway, the demand for coal was greater and more efficient methods of extracting coal were needed. In 1700, about 2.7 million tonnes of coal were mined each year. By 1900 this figure had increased to 250 million tonnes. A hundred years later, world coal production had risen to just over 4 billion tonnes. This represented about 24 per cent of the world's energy consumption.

> **❝** Coal will be providing a substantial proportion of the UK's fuel mix for the generation of electricity in the next decade. Generator demand demonstrates that there has never been a better time to reopen the Hatfield colliery. **❞**
>
> Richard Budge, Chief Executive, Powerfuel UK

▽ An open cast coalmine in Scotland. Diggers excavate the coal from the ground, then large trucks transport it to the power station's crushing plant where it is crushed to a powder.

Open cast mining

The type of coalmine depends on the depth and quality of the seams and the local geology, as well as environmental factors of the area, such as the need to protect wildlife habitats or avoiding the pollution of water supplies.

In some areas the coal seams occur close to the surface. This makes it possible to dig out the coal in an open cast mine. The earth above the coal seam (overburden) is removed, and the coal is dug out using large machines. Once the coal is extracted then the overburden is used to fill the hole.

Deep coalmines

Most coal seams are too deep for open cast mining. Instead, a shaft is dug down to the coal seam, which can be hundreds of metres below the surface. Once the shaft reaches the coal seam, tunnels are dug along the seam and the coal is removed. This type of mining can be dangerous and miners have to face many dangers such as tunnel collapses, flooding and the build up of poisonous gases. Deep mines produce a lot of waste material such as rock and soil, which is dumped above ground, creating unsightly spoil heaps.

Today, the two main types of deep mine are room-and-pillar and longwall. In room-and-pillar mining,

THE ARGUMENT: Coal is a valuable source of energy

For:
- There is a plentiful supply in many parts of the world.
- It releases a lot of energy per tonne.
- Coalmining creates jobs.
- Coal is cheaper than oil and gas.

Against:
- Coal, especially lignite, releases polluting gases when burnt.
- It is bulky to transport, compared with oil and gas.
- Open cast mining creates environmental damage.

the coal is mined by cutting a series of 'rooms' into the coal seam and leaving behind columns or 'pillars' of coal to support the roof of the mine. However, as much as 40 per cent of the coal is left behind during this method. In longwall mining, a large machine cuts the coal and holds up the roof. The coal falls onto a conveyor belt and is removed. When the machine is moved forward, the roof is left to collapse. This method removes 75 per cent of the coal.

Oil and gas formation

Oil has been used as a fuel for more than 5,000 years. The Ancient Sumerians, Assyrians and Babylonians used crude oil and asphalt that leaked out of the ground. The Ancient Egyptians used oil as a medicine for wounds. In North America, Native Americans used blankets to skim oil off the surface of streams and lakes. They used the oil in medicines and to make their canoes waterproof.

From the sea

Oil and gas is formed from the remains of microscopic animals and plants that lived in the sea more than 300 million years ago. When these organisms died, their remains sank to the sea floor and became covered in a layer of mud and silt. Over millions of years, these layers of sediment built up. As more sediment dropped to the sea floor the remains were compressed and formed oil and natural gas. Bubbles of oil and gas seeped through the rock, filling the tiny spaces around the particles of rock. Eventually, the oil and gas reached a layer of impervious (or non-porous) rock through which they could not pass and pockets of oil and gas were formed.

Crude oil

Crude oil is the term used for the 'unprocessed' oil that comes out of the ground. Both crude oil and natural gas are made up of many different substances. For example, crude oil contains substances such as diesel, kerosene and lubricating oils, while natural gas is mostly methane with small amounts of gases such as ethane, propane, butane and pentane. However, the composition of both crude oil and natural gas can vary widely.

THE ARGUMENT: There are many benefits to using oil as fuel

For:
- Oil is a liquid, so it can be pumped from the ground and transported to the refinery.
- Oil contains many different substances, so has many uses.
- It burns more cleanly than coal.

Against:
- Oil spills harm the environment and wildlife.
- When it is burnt, oil releases CO_2 and nitrogen oxides.
- Oil produces more pollution when burnt compared with natural gas.
- Oil is flammable, so can be dangerous to transport and use.

Where is oil and gas found?

The world's largest oil-producing countries are Saudi Arabia, Russia, the United States, Iran and Mexico. The Middle East, South America, Southeast Asia, the North Sea (between the United Kingdom and Norway) and West Africa are other oil-rich regions.

Natural gas is usually found close to oil. The world's largest producer of gas is Russia. Other major producers include Canada, the United States, the United Kingdom and Mexico. Gas is also found near coal beds, providing a relatively cheap energy supply since the beds are usually close to the surface, which makes drilling easier. Nowadays this gas is collected from coalmines and used as a fuel. Since the 1960s, there has been a dramatic increase in the discovery of gas fields, making gas the fastest-growing energy resource. The present global use of natural gas is approximately 20 per cent of all fossil fuel use, and this figure is predicted to rise in the future.

▽ This miner is showing what crude oil looks like when it comes straight out of the ground. Crude oil is often mixed with sand, water and gases.

Extracting and refining oil

For many thousands of years, people collected oil from the surface of the Earth. That changed in 1859, when an American, Edwin Drake, dug a well and struck oil. He worked out how to pump oil to the surface and stored it in wooden barrels. A similar method is still in use today.

Rotary drilling

Today, the most widely used method of drilling for oil is called rotary drilling. The drill and other equipment is supported by a derrick (or drilling rig). The rotary drill works a bit like a screwdriver, turning rapidly to force its way through the ground. The end of the drill is called the bit. This is attached to a drill collar, which in turn is attached to the drill pipe. As the bit turns deeper into the ground, new sections of drill pipe are added.

Drilling fluid is pumped down the inside of the pipe to help break up the rocks and lubricate the drill bit. The drilling fluid and debris (waste) are brought back to the surface outside the drill pipe. Once the drill bit reaches the reserves of oil, the drill pipe is raised and the oil is extracted.

Until the 1970s, most oil wells were vertical. However, new technologies allowed the construction of angled wells, and even horizontal ones.

Horizontal wells are very useful as they are able to pass along a reservoir of oil, rather than through it. This means that more oil can be extracted. Angled wells allow engineers to drill for oil that lies below environmentally sensitive areas, such as wildlife habitats or areas of natural beauty. This is called extended reach drilling.

Refining oil

The crude oil that is pumped straight from the ground contains many different compounds, such as petrol, diesel, kerosene, gas oil, lubricating oils and fuel oils and these compounds vary in thickness.

After the crude oil is transported by pipeline or tanker to an oil refinery, the different compounds are separated.

Dissolved gases make up the thinnest oils, while asphalt is the thickest. The most common way of separating the different fractions of oil is through the process of distillation. During this process, the oil is heated. At certain temperatures, the different compounds boil and become vapours, which are then collected and condensed. For example, kerosene boils at between 180° and 260°C, while fuel oil typically boils at higher temperatures – in excess of 330°C. Some of the fractions of oil may be chemically treated to make other compounds.

Crude oil was discovered under the North Sea during the 1960s. However, the oil fields were located in the most remote northern areas, where there was deep water and very rough seas in winter. Due to the high costs of the technology involved, it did not become economic to extract oil from the North Sea until oil prices rose during the late 1970s.

Since then, the North Sea oil fields have made the UK and Norway two of the world's major oil-producing countries, boosting their economies and reducing their dependence on oil from the Middle East.

△ An oil production platform, North Sea, which is operated by the Occidental Oil company.

The difficult sea conditions meant that new engineering techniques had to be developed. Costs are high; for example, in 2006 it cost up to US$46 million to build and install a new oil platform in the North Sea. Onshore wells cost from US$900,000 to US$14 million. There are more than 100 oil fields in operation in the North Sea; many are small oil fields that have been discovered in the last ten years. Most of the oil reserves belong to the UK and Norway, but some belong to Denmark, Germany and the Netherlands.

CHAPTER 3 Harnessing energy from fossil fuels

It is the carbon in fossil fuels that makes them such valuable sources of energy. Most of the world's coal production is used to generate electricity. However, natural gas is now replacing coal as the preferred fuel as it burns cleaner than coal, which means that it produces less air pollution. For example, natural gas produces between 40 and 50 per cent less CO_2 for the same amount of electricity generated as coal.

▽ Steam billows from the cooling towers of this coal-fired power station that has been fitted with a flue gas desulphurisation unit.

Inside a coal-fired power station

The coal is transported to the power station where it is pulverised into a powder and blown into a boiler. The burning coal heats water that circulates in pipes around the boiler. The water is then turned into steam, which spins the blades of the turbine. As the turbine shaft spins, it drives the generator and this produces electricity. The electricity passes along wires to the transformer where the voltage is increased. The electricity then passes into the national grid for distribution to homes, schools and industry.

Waste gases

The spent steam is cooled so that it condenses back into water and can be re-circulated back to the boiler. The clouds that can be seen escaping from the top of cooling towers are created by steam that escapes and condenses to form water droplets. These clouds are just water. However, the exhaust gases from the boiler leave through a chimney and they may contain gases such as CO_2, sulphur dioxide and nitrous oxide. These are gases that contribute to much of the world's air pollution. Although coal is a very convenient fuel to burn in power stations, it reduces air quality quite significantly. Another waste is the ash left in the boiler. This is used in making concrete and in building roads, although sometimes it is dumped in landfill sites.

Better efficiency

Older designs of coal-fired power station convert about 35 per cent of the energy locked up in coal into electricity. However, newer designs of power station have improved this. One such method involves the gasification of coal. When coal is brought into contact with steam and oxygen, reactions take place that produce gases such as carbon monoxide and hydrogen. These gases can be used to power gas turbines. Gasification can increase the efficiency to more than 50 per cent, as well as produce less solid waste and lower emissions of CO_2, sulphur dioxide and nitrogen oxides. A process called Integrated Coal Gasification Combined Cycle (IGCC) increases the efficiency further by using the waste heat from the gases to produce steam to drive a steam turbine, as well as a gas turbine.

CASE STUDY: Coal powers China

China is dependent on coal because it provides 80 per cent of the country's electricity. The rest of its energy comes from either nuclear or hydropower. China's economy is growing at such a rate that it plans to build more than 500 new coal-fired power stations over the next couple of decades. Already China is the world's second largest producer of CO_2 and this huge expansion in the number of power stations will increase the emissions further. Another problem is that most of China's coal is low-grade brown coal. This type of coal releases sulphur dioxide when burnt. Unless the power stations are fitted with flue gas desulphurisation filters, damage from acid rain also increases.

△ Filling up cars with petrol or diesel is becoming increasingly expensive. Diesel cars are more fuel-efficient than petrol cars, as they are able to run further on a litre of fuel.

Burning oil in vehicles

Oil has many uses, but one of the most important of these is in vehicle engines. Engines carry out work; for example, a car engine transforms the energy locked up in a fuel into movement energy. This energy conversion takes place within the car engine, so it is described as an internal combustion engine. This is in contrast to an external combustion engine, such as a steam engine, in which the fuel is burnt outside the engine to produce steam, which then drives the engine.

Four-stroke engines

Most car engines use a four-stroke combustion cycle, invented in 1867. There are four parts to the cycle:

1. The intake valve opens and the piston moves down to allow a mix of air and fuel into the cylinder.
2. The piston moves back up and squashes the fuel mix. This is the compression stroke.
3. The spark plug produces a spark that ignites the fuel. The fuel explodes and the piston is then forced down.
4. Then the exhaust valve opens and the exhaust gases leave the cylinder.

In the engine, the piston is attached to the crankshaft. The up-and-down movement of the piston turns the crankshaft, which turns the wheels. Modern car engines have four or six cylinders in order to produce enough force to power a car's movement.

Different engines

There are two main types of car engine – petrol and diesel. The difference between the two engines is the fuel that the engines burn, and the way that the fuel is introduced into the engine and ignited.

In a diesel engine, the compression stroke compresses only air and not fuel. There is no spark in this process. Instead, the compression of the air generates enough heat to ignite the fuel when it is injected into the cylinder. Diesel is heavier and oilier than petrol.

There is more energy locked up in the heavier diesel fuel, so a litre of diesel produces more energy than a litre of petrol. This means that when diesel burns, it releases about 30 per cent more energy than petrol, so a diesel engine can run further on a litre of fuel than a petrol engine.

Diesel fuel is also cheaper to refine. In the past, diesel engines were powerful, reliable and economical but they were also noisy and produced a lot of sooty particles in the exhaust fumes. For this reason they tended to be used in commercial vehicles such as vans and lorries rather than in cars. However, over the last 20 years or so, diesel engines have improved and many modern cars now have diesel engines.

CASE STUDY: Liquefied petroleum gas

Liquefied petroleum gas (or LPG) is an alternative fuel to petrol or diesel. It is a cleaner burning fuel, and produces significantly less air pollution compared with other fuels. LPG contains either butane or propane gases. These gases exist as liquids only at very low temperatures or under pressure. LPG is stored under pressure as a liquid in a tank within the car.

When the pressure is released the liquid boils and forms a gas. This gas is used to power the car. Car engines powered by LPG fuels are just as powerful as car engines running on diesel or petrol, but they are very quiet and produce far fewer polluting emissions. LPG is becoming more popular and it is now possible to convert a diesel or petrol engine to run on LPG.

CHAPTER 4 Environment and resources

Each year, an average-sized coal-fired power station produces about 11 million tonnes of CO_2, 29,000 tonnes of nitrogen oxide, 16,000 tonnes of sulphur dioxide, 1 million tonnes of ash, 1,000 tonnes of dust, as well as 500,000 tonnes of gypsum and 21,000 tonnes of sludge.

The gases contribute to air pollution and environmental problems, such as acid rain, smog and global warming. Gypsum and ash are solid waste that have to be disposed of safely. Some gypsum is used in building supplies.

▽ These conifer trees are suffering from acid rain damage. They have dropped their needles and the branches are showing signs of die-back.

Acid rain

Coal is a dirty fuel compared with oil and gas because it contains impurities such as sulphur. When it burns, the sulphur reacts with oxygen in the air, producing sulphur dioxide – a major contributor to acid rain.

Acid rain has many effects. It erodes stone, especially the limestone and sandstone used in buildings. It also damages trees. Conifer trees are particularly vulnerable as they tend to grow on thin, acidic soils that are easily damaged by acid rain. The acid rain causes their needles to die and drop off. Acid rain also drains into watercourses such as streams, rivers and lakes and makes the water more acidic. This harms aquatic animals, especially fish and amphibians.

Preventing acid rain

Sulphur dioxide emissions from power stations can be reduced by fitting special filters in the chimney to absorb the sulphur dioxide gas. This is called flue gas desulphurisation. In the EU and the United States there are strict laws that control the emissions from power stations. Many large power stations, for example Drax in England, have fitted flue gas filter systems in order to meet the new regulations.

Another way to reduce sulphur dioxide emissions is to switch from burning coal to burning gas as it produces little sulphur dioxide and even less CO_2.

Carbon dioxide

Power stations also emit CO_2, the greenhouse gas that traps heat in the atmosphere. Scientists believe that warming of the lower atmosphere by just a few degrees could cause enormous climate changes, resulting in more extreme weather events such as hurricanes, tornadoes, floods and droughts. When water is heated, it expands. This is called thermal expansion. Therefore a slight increase in the temperature of seawater causes it to expand. Thermal expansion has already raised sea levels by as much as 20 centimetres over the last 100 years. This is combined with the effect of melting glaciers and polar ice caps. In time, low-lying land areas, especially in Bangladesh, Florida and islands such as the Maldives could be flooded.

Damaging the ozone layer

Another emission from burning fossil fuels is nitrogen oxide. About 40 per cent of it in the atmosphere comes from burning fossil fuels in power stations and from cars. Nitrogen oxide reacts with water in the atmosphere to produce acid rain, but it also damages the ozone layer. The ozone layer, high up in the atmosphere, acts as a shield from the Sun, filtering out harmful ultraviolet (UV) radiation. Damage to the ozone layer lets more UV radiation through and can cause skin cancers.

CASE STUDY: Drax power station

The largest fossil-fuelled power station in Europe is Drax, located in Yorkshire, England. Drax has six generators, producing around 4,000 megawatts of electricity – equivalent to 7 per cent of the UK's electricity needs. It is also the UK's cleanest and most efficient power plant. It burns coal and has a desulphurisation unit that removes 90 per cent of the sulphur dioxide.

Drax produces more electricity per tonne of coal than other power stations because of its advanced control systems. Scientists at Drax are experimenting with burning a mixture of coal and petroleum coke to reduce CO_2 emissions. Petroleum coke is a carbon-rich solid formed at the end of the oil refining process. It releases a lot of energy when it is burnt but it does contain sulphur.

Pollution from transport

Transport is powered by oil. Motor vehicles, aircraft, trains and ships all rely on a liquid fuel derived from oil. When this fuel is burnt, it produces a mix of gases including CO_2, nitrogen, water vapour, nitrogen oxides and sulphur dioxide. The demand for transport is increasing. In 2006, the world vehicle fleet was about 800 million, of which 37 per cent of the vehicles were in the US. They are all contributing to the rise in CO_2 levels in the atmosphere.

CASE STUDY: Low sulphur fuels

In recent years there has been a switch from normal diesel and petrol fuels to ultra-low sulphur fuel. Ultra-low sulphur diesel contains less than 50 parts per million of sulphur, while normal conventional diesel may contain as much as 500 parts per million of sulphur. This means there is less sulphur dioxide in the exhaust fumes, and the fuel produces fewer sooty particles which blacken buildings, cause acid rain and have been linked to diseases such as asthma and cancer.

Cleaning up emissions

Catalytic converters can be placed in a vehicle's exhaust system to remove much of the carbon monoxide, hydrocarbons and nitrogen oxides. Sunlight breaks down the hydrocarbons to form oxidants, which react with nitrogen oxides to cause low-level ozone (O_3), a major component of smog. Nitrogen oxides contribute to both smog and acid rain and are also irritants that can cause human respiratory problems.

Hybrid cars

Catalytic converters do not remove CO_2. The way to reduce emissions of CO_2 is by burning less fuel. In general, a car with a small engine burns less fuel. However, many people are more concerned about a car's performance than its CO_2 emissions, so do not buy cars with small engines as they do not perform so well.

A different approach is the hybrid car – which is a cross between a traditional car with a four-stroke engine (see page 20) and a car with an electric motor and battery. Hybrid cars are powered by both systems. At low speeds, when less power is needed, the car is powered by the electric motor, but at higher speeds the petrol engine kicks in. Hybrid engines are more efficient than traditional car engines, so they can travel further on a litre of petrol.

△ The Toyota Prius is a hybrid car that is popular in California. California has some of the strictest emissions regulations in the world.

Some hybrid cars are up to 35 per cent more efficient than the equivalent model with a petrol engine. As a result, emissions are also much lower. The benefit is greatest at low speeds when the electric motor is running as there are no emissions. This is very important in cities as hybrid cars use their motors when stuck in traffic. Hybrids also have advantages over electric cars. The battery in an electric car has to be charged, but the battery in the hybrid car is charged by the petrol engine, so there is no risk of becoming stranded with a flat battery.

THE ARGUMENT: We should all be driving hybrid cars

For:
- Hybrid cars have lower polluting emissions.
- They are more fuel-efficient.
- They cause less noise pollution as the motor is almost silent.

Against:
- Hybrid cars cost more than conventional cars.
- A hybrid car's battery needs replacing about every ten years.
- They are slower to accelerate than a similar-sized conventional car.

Land use

The extraction of fossil fuels, especially coal, can damage large areas of countryside. Also, more land is lost to new roads and ports that are built to service the new mine or oil field.

Land use and coalmining

Open cast mining spoils large tracts of countryside. For example, in Germany there are vast open cast lignite mines and whole villages have been dug up, leaving behind holes in the ground.

A well planned open cast operation involves removing the soil and the overburden and storing them separately. They can then be used to refill the hole once the coal is removed and the area can be restored to its former use or given a new use. Sometimes, the land has to be levelled and acidic soils treated with lime and fertilizer so that plants will grow. Former open cast mines can also be used as landfill sites for rubbish.

In some regions, such as the Appalachian mountains in the United States, whole mountain peaks have been removed using explosives and the overburden pushed into nearby valleys. This flattens the land and gives the miners access to the coal. However, the environmental damage of this operation is widespread; for example, forests are cleared and river courses changed.

CASE STUDY:
Mining and the Appalachian mountains

There are thick coal seams under the Appalachian range. As a result of rising coal prices and changes in laws, mining companies want to dig more mines in the mountains. However, these companies use a technique known as mountain peak removal and this is having a huge effect on the environment of the mountains. Already thousands of hectares of forest have been cleared and hundreds of mountain ridges have been blown apart.

Almost 2,000 kilometres of water courses have been buried under piles of rock. Huge slurry ponds threaten local communities. In 2000, a slurry pond in Kentucky spilled about 1,500 million litres of coal sludge into two mountain streams. All aquatic life in both of the streams died, and drinking water supplies were affected over hundreds of kilometres to the Ohio river. Some rivers were so polluted that the water was black for weeks.

The coal is transported to a processing plant where it is washed. The waste from this process is stored in earthen dams containing millions of litres of slurry. Often these slurry ponds are ignored, with devastating consequences. In 1972, the dam around a slurry pond broke and flooded a valley near Buffalo Creek, West Virginia, US, killing 125 people.

Deep mines can also scar the landscape. During the mining process, rock from around the coal seam and low-grade coal is brought to the surface and piled nearby to create a spoil heap. These wastes are usually very acidic and contain high levels of metal salts, creating conditions in

which plants cannot grow. Any water draining off this waste may also be polluted. Restoration involves the landscaping of waste heaps as well as treating the acidic soils.

Land for oil and gas
Onshore oil and gas fields can also cause the loss of valuable habitats, although not as much as coalmines. If permission has been given to drill for oil in wildlife areas or other sensitive areas, angled wells may be drilled from outside of the area.

Often the oil is piped to a port for transporting around the world. The building of oil storage tanks and associated buildings can result in the loss of valuable estuarine or mangrove habitats. Also, there is a maintenance zone around the pipelines, which may occupy further areas of land.

▽ Large areas of mangrove swamp have been cleared in Australia to make way for oil storage depots and associated industries.

Cost and investment

Fossil fuels have been the main energy source in power stations for more than 100 years. As a result, the technology is well understood and advanced. The cost of the raw material (not taking into account environmental costs) remains relatively cheap.

Fossil fuels versus renewables

Large power stations have a lot of buying power and can use this to make savings. For example, large quantities of fuel are purchased and lower prices can be negotiated. Therefore, the cost of generating electricity from fossil fuels is cheaper than using renewable sources of energy such as wind, solar or water. However, the cost advantage of fossil fuels changes when the environmental costs are considered.

> **"** The threat of global climate change and the warnings about energy security will force Europe to drastically change and diversify its sources of supply, relying more and more on renewable energy. **"**
>
> European Commission Report, 2004

Using biomass

Some small-scale power stations have been built which use biomass fuels; for example, the waste litter from poultry farms, and wood from fast-growing plants such as willow. Biomass fuels are bulky and their energy content is less than an equivalent mass of coal, so they tend to be difficult and expensive to transport. They have to be used locally to avoid these costs. However, these crops are easy to grow and harvest with little damage to the environment. In fact, willow crops tend to attract many insects and birds. Poultry litter is considerably cheaper than coal but there is a limited supply, and it is particularly bulky, so the power plant has to be built in areas where there is poultry farming.

Taxing CO_2

Another important consideration is a tax on CO_2 emissions. It is likely that governments will tax industries that release CO_2 to reduce emissions. This could double the cost of generating electricity from fossil fuels and would bring the costs in line with those of using renewable energy sources.

◁ Power stations, with their cooling towers and coal stores, occupy large areas of land and require good road and rail communications.

THE ARGUMENT: We should invest in renewables

For:
- Renewables provide a never-ending source of energy.
- They make use of waste materials, such as poultry litter in the case of biomass power.
- Renewables are ideal for use in local, small-scale power stations or microgeneration in people's homes and buildings. For example, solar panels can be fitted to homes.
- Renewable energy sources are better for the environment as they give off less CO_2.

Against:
- Currently it costs more to generate electricity from renewable sources such as water, the wind and Sun than from fossil fuels.
- A continuous supply of energy from the wind or Sun cannot be guaranteed.
- Biomass crops are bulky. This makes them both difficult and expensive to transport over long distances.
- The energy content of biomass is less than an equivalent mass of coal.

Future power stations

As demand for electricity increases, the electricity generating companies need to make the decision to either modify the existing power stations to enable them to generate more electricity, or to build new ones.

Building new plants

Most of the larger power stations have a steam turbine (see page 18) with the fossil fuel releasing heat to generate steam. However, over the last 20 years or so, other designs of power station have been built. The availability of natural gas has meant that many of the newer plants use gas turbines – resulting in fewer emissions.

△ One of the 500 new coal-fired power stations being built in China to meet the country's increasing demands for electricity.

Added to this, the gas turbine is more efficient than a steam turbine that is powered by coal. The cheapest type of power station – and one of the most efficient – is a combined-cycle gas turbine. The hot waste gases from the turbine are used to produce steam that powers a second turbine. This use of waste heat energy increases the efficiency levels to more than 50 per cent. In North America or Europe the cost of this type of power station to supply about a million homes is between US$665 and 760 million.

Modifying old power stations

New power stations are very costly to build so it can be cheaper to use new technology to improve existing power stations. For example, by using a new design of turbine or new mixes of fuel to increase the amount of energy released. Power stations can be cleaned up by the fitting of flue gas desulphurisation filters in the chimneys (see page 22). It is also possible to modify a coal-fired power station so that all CO_2 emissions are captured. This process is known as 'clean coal technology' and was developed in Australia. The coal is burnt in pure oxygen and the CO_2 is then collected and pumped deep below ground into saline water-bearing rocks or depleted oil fields. However, the long-term effects of this method are uncertain.

Nuclear power stations

Another type of power plant is the nuclear power station, fuelled by uranium rather than fossil fuels. The cost to build one of the latest designs of nuclear power station can range from US$650 to US$1.5 billion – a huge investment. However, the energy yield per tonne of uranium is far greater than that of fossil fuel. For example, a 1,000-megawatt nuclear power station requires about 74 kilogrammes of fuel per day; while an equivalent-sized, coal-fired plant needs about 8,600 tonnes of coal per day. There are no CO_2 emissions from nuclear energy, but radioactive waste must be stored safely for hundreds of years. For this reason, many countries that have the technology to build nuclear power stations prefer to invest in renewable energy sources.

THE ARGUMENT: We should build new fossil fuel-powered power stations

For:
- Power stations provide a reliable source of electricity for domestic and industrial use.
- They provide jobs.

Against:
- Clearance of land for new power stations and coal stores, approach roads and railways causes loss of wildlife habitats.
- The power stations create air pollution from burning coal.
- They create solid waste that has to be disposed of.
- As fossil fuels are depleted and their cost rises, an investment in new power stations may not be profitable.

Transporting fossil fuels

Once the fossil fuels have been extracted from below the ground, they need to be transported to power stations and oil refineries.

Moving coal

Coal is a bulky fuel so it is usually moved by train across land. In many places, power stations are built close to the coalmines so that the distances are short. However, some countries lack any coal reserves and so their coal supplies are imported by rail or by sea.

Moving oil

Oil is usually piped to a collecting area and from there it is either moved into a network of pipelines or transferred to large oil tankers and moved by sea. There are about 3,500 oil tankers currently in operation, the largest of which are equipped to carry as much as half a million tonnes of crude oil.

Oil is a harmful substance if it is spilt into the environment. As it is a liquid, it can seep into watercourses. The loading and unloading of oil at ports is a risky operation. Most ports use barriers and other methods to minimise any spill – should it occur. However, the greatest risk is the oil tanker having an accident at sea, causing large amounts of oil to pour into the sea. Some oil tankers are fitted with a double hull. This means that if the outer hull is damaged, the inner hull protects the ship and also prevents an oil spillage. However, tankers have a very long lifespan and there are still some single-hulled oil tankers in use that were built in the 1960s and 1970s. Fortunately nowadays, their access to some coastal waters, such as Prince William Sound in Alaska, is restricted.

Moving gas

Gas is usually piped from the gas fields to the end users via various storage facilities. Some of the gas pipelines are long; for example, some pipelines run all the way from Central Asia to Europe. As natural gas becomes an increasingly important fuel in the world today, more pipelines are planned. For example, in 2002 the government of Afghanistan signed an agreement to build an 850-kilometre pipeline that would carry gas from Turkmenistan to Pakistan and India.

> " Modern society will find no solution to the ecological problem unless it takes a serious look at its lifestyle. "
>
> Pope John Paul II, 1990

△ Cleaning up an oil spill. Although unsightly, some scientists argue that it is best to leave the oil and let natural processes break it down.

CASE STUDY:
Exxon oil spill

One of the worst oil spills occurred in 1989 when the oil tanker *Exxon Valdez* hit a reef outside Valdez in Alaska, spilling its oil into Prince William Sound. Three days later a huge storm pushed the oil further afield, affecting 1,900 kilometres of Alaskan coastline. Exxon claims that 40,900 cubic metres of oil were spilled in the accident, but many environmental organisations believe the oil spill to be as much as 110,000 cubic metres.

A huge clean up operation took place but not in time to save the lives of many thousands of animals, including about 250,000 sea birds, 2,800 sea otters, 300 harbour seals, 250 bald eagles, up to 22 orcas, and billions of salmon and herring eggs. Although signs of the oil spill were gone within a year, the effects can still be felt. There has been a significant decline in the numbers of many marine animals such as sea otters, ducks and pink salmon.

Exploring for oil and gas

Most of the world's large oil and gas fields have been discovered. Now oil companies are looking for new reserves in increasingly remote areas such as the Arctic, the Sahara and beneath some oceans. The oil company BP is currently exploring in Alaska, while the Premier Oil company is exploring for oil beneath the Western Sahara.

Although costs are high, oil companies are investing billions of dollars into exploration and production. It is estimated that as much as US$800 billion will be needed by 2013 to develop existing reserves as well as exploration costs, estimated at about US$240 billion a year. For example, offshore wells are very expensive to drill. In 2005, it cost about US$37,000 per day to rent an offshore rig to drill a new oil well. It usually takes about 45 days to drill a new oil or gas well,

△ Carrying out a geophysical survey in the Sahara to locate new oil fields.

so it can cost up to about US$1.7 million. Following this, a production platform is brought in, costing around US$9 million or more.

> **Developing a small section of Arctic National Wildlife Refuge would not only create thousands of new jobs, but it would eventually reduce our dependence on foreign oil by up to a million barrels of oil a day.**
>
> US president, George W. Bush, 2005

New oil fields

Once a new oil reserve is found, it can take several years or more to bring the first oil to market. The oil field has to be mapped, test wells drilled and then drilling rigs brought in. Then pipelines and storage facilities need to be constructed. Finally, the oil has to be shipped to the oil refinery.

Some of the new oil fields may never be developed because of the high costs involved in extraction. Even if the price of oil rose, there would be an accompanying increase in the costs of plastics, steel and transportation. Although the oil underground may have increased in value, the cost of extracting it has also increased.

There are many other reasons why oil reserves are not exploited. For example, Florida in the US has oil reserves but they have not been developed because people are concerned that oil production is not compatible with tourism. Sometimes, there are environmental reasons why the oil cannot be extracted. One of the most controversial oil fields lies under the Arctic National Wildlife Refuge, a huge wilderness area in northern Alaska. It is one of the most important wildlife areas in the Arctic. However, the Refuge lies to the east of Prudhoe Bay, the Unites States' largest oil field and research has shown that substantial oil reserves lie beneath the Refuge. This pristine environment is under threat from the oil industry. The final decision as to whether to extract the oil has to be made by the senate of the United States.

THE ARGUMENT: The US should exploit oil from the Arctic National Wildlife Refuge

For:
- Directional drilling would allow oil to be extracted by disturbing only 1 per cent of the refuge.
- Less than 0.01 per cent of the land area would be affected.
- Drilling in the Arctic would reduce US dependency on foreign oil.
- Hundreds of thousands of jobs could be created directly or indirectly.

Against:
- The US should rather spend their money on renewable power and combating CO_2 emissions.
- Drilling in the Arctic could make it easier for oil companies to exploit other wilderness areas.
- The drilling would interfere with the herds of caribou on which people depend for food.
- Any oil spill would severely damage the environment and its effects would be long lasting.

Alternative fossil fuels

Coal, gas and oil are the main forms of fossil fuels but are not the only ones. There are other fossil fuels such as peat, tar sands and oil shales. With the right technology, these could be put to greater use in the future.

Peat

Peat is a soft, brown material made from compressed and partially decomposed vegetation. It forms in a waterlogged habitat such as a swamp or bog. It has about 50 per cent carbon content and can be dried and burnt as a fuel. However, it does not burn as efficiently as coal.

One of the main problems with peat is the loss of valuable wetland habitats known as bogs. In order to extract the peat, the bog is lost. Hand-cutting of peat is a slow and labour-intensive process, but it can allow the bog to recover partially. In contrast, large-scale mechanised extraction processes drain and strip all vegetation from vast expanses of bog, often completely destroying the habitat.

Oil shales

Oil shales are rocks that are rich in an organic material called kerogen. Oil shales can be burnt as a poor quality coal but usually they are processed to produce oil. They are crushed and heated to between 445° and 500°C without any oxygen. This is called pyrolysis. The kerogen within the rock

▽ Peat is dug by hand and left to dry, then it is sold locally as an alternative fuel to coal.

CASE STUDY: Oil from coal

During World War II (1939–1945), Germany developed a technique for extracting oil from coal because there was a shortage of crude oil. Today, a leader in this field is South Africa, a country with rich coal reserves but little oil. The coal-to-oil process has been modernised by the oil company Sasol. Although this process could supply large quantities of oil, it is not without its problems. Coal-to-oil fuels become cost-effective only when oil prices exceed US$37 a barrel (160 litres).

However, the coal-to-oil process is also environmentally damaging because considerable CO_2 is released during the production of the fuel, as well as when it is burnt. In fact, twice as much CO_2 is produced than is released from an equivalent amount of petrol derived from crude oil. Coal-to-oil may become more common in the future and the benefits of this new source of oil have to be weighed against the increased emissions of CO_2 and how this affects global warming.

breaks down and forms oil. However, the mining, transporting and processing of oil shale is an energy-hungry process, so up to 40 per cent of the potential energy locked up in the shale is used in oil production.

The world's oil shale reserves could yield as much as 400 trillion litres of oil. Of this, about 150 trillion litres are located in the United States. Oil shales are mined in Estonia, Russia, Brazil and China but until recently, mining was in decline because of the economic and environmental problems associated with open cast mining. Also, the extraction of oil produces large quantities of ash and waste rock, which have to be carefully disposed of. However, as oil prices rise, the large-scale mining of oil shale may become more economically viable.

Tar sands

These are sands that contain bitumen, a heavy oil. The largest deposits, found in Canada, contain an estimated 250 trillion million litres of oil. However, extracting the oil is costly and damaging to the environment. Surface sands are dug from open cast mines and crushed to extract the oil. Deeper deposits are extracted by pumping steam into the ground to create a slurry. At the extraction plant, the bitumen is skimmed off the top.

CHAPTER 6 | A fossil fuel-powered future?

How long will the fossil fuels last? Everyone agrees that there is a limited supply of coal, gas and oil, although not all agree about how much of them are left. However, it is clear that we have to find ways of making fossil fuels last longer.

How much gas?

Global reserves of gas at the end of 2005 stood at 180 million million cubic metres, of which about 75 per cent lie in Europe, Russia, Central Asia, and the Middle East. The reserves have increased by 25 per cent since 1995, but consumption has increased by a similar percentage. Gas production is likely to peak in about 2030. This is the point at which the gas-producing countries reach their maximum output, and then output starts to decline. Other sources of natural gas, such as landfill and organic wastes, could be exploited in the future.

How much oil?

Oil reserves have increased by more than 50 per cent in the last 22 years and are expected to continue to increase as more oil is discovered. In 2006, global oil reserves were estimated at about 1,300 billion barrels, of which about two-thirds lay in the Middle East and Canada.

There are many estimates of when peak oil production will be reached. A French government report suggested that peak oil production will be in about 2013. This is based on a 3 per cent increase in demand each year and discoveries of new oil fields with reserves of 10 billion barrels per year. Oil consumption per day would reach a maximum of around 97 million barrels per day. Other estimates suggest that the peak will be later, somewhere between 2020 and 2030.

How much coal?

Coal resources are estimated to be ten times larger than oil reserves and may last several hundred years. It is also thought that the large quantity of coal waste that is stored near the coalmines could become exploitable with the use of new technology.

Saving energy

Fossil fuels could last much longer if they were used carefully. The efficiency of power stations could be increased so more electricity was produced from every tonne of fossil fuel. Consumers could reduce their consumption of electricity by using low-energy appliances. Car engines could be more efficient so that they travelled further on a litre of fuel, while efficient, cheap

△ Fuel cell-powered buses are appearing in many cities such as Stockholm, Sweden.

and reliable public transportation systems may encourage more people to leave their cars at home.

An example of energy savings is happening in Southampton, England, where waste heat from power generation is used to heat buildings. The city has integrated a geothermal source of hot water with a combined heat and power generator producing 5.7 megawatts of electricity, as well as hot water. Many thousands of buildings in the city are connected to the district's heating scheme.

❝ What is very important is conservation, especially in transport. Raising taxes on fuel, introducing toll roads and bridges into major cities for example, but also stopping the spreading of suburbs ever further from city centres. Controlling suburban blight is one way to slow oil consumption until we are a society no longer dependent on oil. ❞

Deborah White, Senior Energy analyst, Société Générale, Paris

CASE STUDY: OPEC

The Organisation of the Petroleum Exporting Countries (OPEC) is an intergovernmental organisation set up in 1960. It has many aims, which include:

- the coordination of oil policies of the member states
- stabilisation of oil prices in order to secure a steady supply of oil to customers
- provision of a regular and fair income to the oil producers and others that invest in the industry.

OPEC's members control about two-thirds of the world's oil reserves and supply 40 per cent of the world's oil production. Decisions made by OPEC regarding the volume of oil being produced have had a considerable influence on world oil prices. For example, in 1973 OPEC started an oil crisis when its members refused to ship oil

△ Representatives of the 11 members of OPEC meet regularly to consider changes in the world's oil markets and ensure that there is a balance between output and demand.

to those countries that had supported Israel in their war against Egypt and Syria. Oil prices rose and there were petrol shortages in many MEDCs. This lead to considerable investment in renewable energies, for example in the United States there was a great expansion of wind farms and solar power plants. However, interest in renewables waned once the oil prices dropped back again. The surge in prices since 2004 has led to new interest in renewables. During the last ten years or so, the influence of OPEC has decreased as oil production from non-OPEC members has increased; for example oil can now be supplied from the Gulf of Mexico and the North Sea.

THE ARGUMENT: Governments should control oil prices

For:
- By pricing their own oil, governments are given the ability to price oil so that it suits their country's current economic situation.
- Governments can increase oil prices to reduce consumption.
- If governments price oil, they can prevent oil companies making large profits.

Against:
- Oil can be used as a political tool. For example, by reducing the oil price, governments would be more popular with voters, especially as energy prices rise.
- If governments made oil cheaper, this would reduce the investment in alternative energy sources.

Oil and politics

Governments are starting to plan for a future where coal, gas and oil may not be so readily available and will cost much more. Forward planning is essential as it can take decades to build new power stations and establish alternative energy sources.

The rising cost of oil

During 2005 and 2006 the price of oil rose to record highs. There were many reasons for this increase. Oil prices usually rise during times of instability in oil-producing countries, as there is a fear of supplies being cut. However, the main force that drives the cost of oil is demand. It has been estimated that world oil demand is set to increase by 47 per cent between 2003 and 2030. Much of the increase is due to the fast-expanding economies of India, China and other Asian countries. However, the supply of oil cannot keep up as most of the oil producers are working at full capacity. Only Saudi Arabia has spare capacity to increase its production. Also, there is an increased demand for the high quality, light crude oils that are used to produce the clean-burning fuels used in cars, whereas most of the spare capacity is for heavier oils.

> What we human beings are all living now ... is an extraordinary but exceptionally dangerous adventure. We have a very small number of years left to fail or to succeed in providing a sustainable future to our species.

Jacques Cousteau, French underwater explorer and author

Securing supplies

Many regions have no natural supplies of fossil fuels of their own so they are reliant on supplies from other countries. For example, the EU is a net importer of energy, and by 2020 about two-thirds of the EU's total energy requirements will be imported. This means as much as 75 per cent of its natural gas supplies could be imported from countries such as Russia.

Countries with large reserves of oil and gas have a lot of political weight. By increasing or decreasing the supply of fuel they can influence the world economy. For example, Russia has huge reserves of coal, gas and oil. Already people have accused Russia of using energy as a political tool to further its influence, especially with countries of the former Soviet Union.

In January 2006, a dispute over gas prices led to the Russian gas company cutting off gas supplies to the Ukraine. The Russians wanted to increase the cost of gas from US$45 to US$200 per 1,000 cubic metres, claiming this was the market price. The Ukraine refused and demanded a phased price rise. Many believed that this was political because of the Ukraine government's close links with the EU. In contrast, Belarus, another former Soviet state, continued to be supplied with gas at US$45 per 1,000 cubic metres.

Around the world, many countries are looking to secure alternative supplies to reduce the risk of interruptions to their oil and gas supplies.

New pipelines

In 2006, the new Baku-Tbilisi-Ceyhan crude oil pipeline was opened. It runs 1,700 kilometres, from Baku, the capital of Azerbaijan, through Georgia and to the port of Ceyhan in Turkey.

A new gas pipeline is also planned. The 3,300-kilometre Nabucco gas pipeline will run from Turkey to Austria. Construction is expected to start in 2008 and be completed by 2011, at a cost of over US$4 billion. It will pipe as much as 30 billion cubic metres of gas from countries such as Iran, Azerbaijan and Turkmenistan. These oil and gas pipelines will reduce the EU's dependence on oil and gas from the Middle East and Russia, and will provide a boost to the economies of Azerbaijan, Georgia and Turkey.

Alternative oil supplies

Some countries are turning to alternative oil sources. For example, oil production using the Canadian tar sands in Alberta has increased by more than 60 per cent since 2002. Oil from tar sands is difficult to extract, but just extracting the most accessible 10 per cent would yield 28 trillion litres of oil.

△ During the Gulf War (1990–1991), the retreating Iraqi army set light to many oil wells in Kuwait. This created clouds of thick black smoke.

CASE STUDY:
Terrorist targets

Any interruption in supply of gas or oil to a country could have severe consequences on that country's economy and political leadership. Therefore it is not surprising that oil and gas pipelines are fast becoming terrorist targets. Pipelines are vulnerable to attack because they are difficult to protect. They run for thousands of kilometres and cannot be protected along their entire length. Some pipelines are built underground. This offers some protection, but there are vulnerable points above ground. Already pipelines in the Caucasus, Nigeria, Colombia, Sudan and Yemen are regularly blown up, while oil facilities have been attacked in countries such as India, Pakistan, Indonesia, Argentina and Ecuador. In Georgia, the new oil pipeline is protected by anti-terrorist units that patrol the pipeline, but they will be unable to protect the pipeline from missile attacks from nearby Iran. An attack could lead to huge oil spills that could harm wildlife and contaminate water supplies, as well as interrupt supplies to the EU.

Looking to the future

Fossil fuels are part of our modern lives. However the supply is limited and the world will have to become less dependent on fossil fuels. New discoveries, the mining of oil shales and tar sands, and improved fuel efficiency will all help to extend the life of fossil fuels. Although experts disagree as to when these fossil fuels will run out, they are all agreed that they will run out, eventually. Before this happens, other sources of energy such as the Sun, wind, water and nuclear power will have to be developed to take the place of fossil fuels. It is going to take decades to develop these energy sources so it is imperative that this process starts soon.

Combating global warming

It is not just the limited supply that will force people to shift away from fossil fuels. Fossil fuels are a major contributor to global warming. If we are to fight climate change by reducing CO_2 emissions, we will have to start applying clean coal technology, use renewable energy sources, and reduce the amount of oil burnt by the millions of vehicles on our roads.

Making difficult decisions

Combating climate change will mean making difficult and, possibly, unpopular decisions. For example, to reduce the polluting emissions from

" Because renewables do not use fossil fuels [most are entirely fuel-free] they are largely immune to the threat of future oil or gas shortages and fossil fuel price hikes. For the same reason, because most renewable technologies require no combustion, they are far kinder to the environment than coal, oil, and natural gas. Smog and acid rain could be eliminated with renewables. The collective lungs of America could breathe a sigh of relief. "

John J. Berger, environmental science and policy consultant, US

vehicles, governments may decide to place heavy taxes on larger makes of car. California has already legislated that any cars driven in the state must meet strict emission controls, and it is very likely other governments may follow this lead.

In order to generate enough electricity to meet the increasing demand, large areas of land or sea may have to be covered by wind turbines or huge tidal barrages, built across their estuaries.

Going nuclear?

It is also possible that governments will build new nuclear power stations. Although nuclear power does not generate any greenhouse gases, it does create radioactive waste that will need to be stored for hundreds of years.

Scientists are currently developing new designs of nuclear power station that will recycle their own radioactive waste. However, the designs are still experimental and it may be some time before a commercial nuclear power station of this design could be built and come into operation.

Governments can legislate to bring about change, but the ordinary person also has an important role to play. If everybody reduced their electricity consumption by just a few per cent, or used public transport rather than their car just once a week, the overall effect would be significant. Action now needs to be taken. Perhaps it will take a major climate crisis such as global warming to make people take action and change their lifestyles?

▽ Although hydroelectric power is a sustainable source of energy, the construction of dams has a considerable impact on the environment.

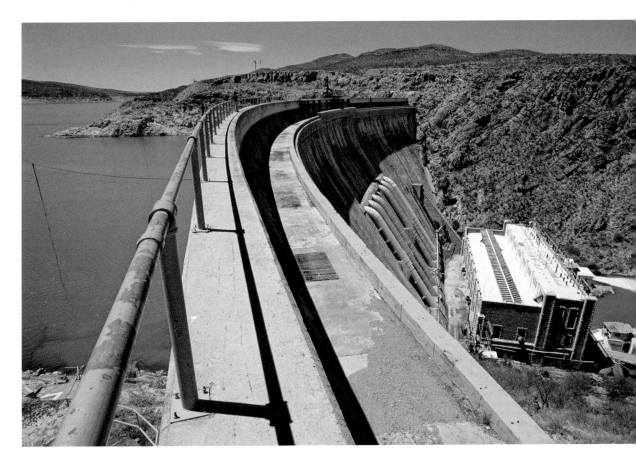

Glossary

Acid rain Rain that has a pH of less than 5.6, due to the formation of sulphuric, nitric and other acids.

Asphalt A sticky, dark substance produced from crude oil residues.

Barrel The unit for measuring oil. One barrel is approximately 159 litres.

Combustion The process of burning in air; it takes place in car engines.

Compression Making something smaller by applying pressure.

Distillation Heating a liquid to its boiling point, then condensing it and collecting the vapour.

Emission The release of a substance into the environment.

Exhaust The hot gases released from an engine as waste products.

Fossil fuel The fuels peat, coal, crude oil and natural gas.

Gasification The process by which coal is turned into a gas.

Generator A machine that produces electricity.

Global warming The gradual warming of the Earth's surface.

Indigenous Peoples or plants that are native to a particular area.

Microscopic Too small to be seen. Only visible using a microscope.

Motor A machine that converts electrical energy into mechanical energy.

Non-renewable Resources that cannot be replaced or replenished, for example the fossil fuels coal, oil and gas.

Overburden The layer of rock and soil that covers a mineral deposit such as a coal seam.

Peak production A point in time when oil-producing countries reach their maximum output; after this time production starts to decline.

Refinery An industrial plant that processes crude oil or metal ores.

Renewable Resources that are able to be replaced or replenished.

Sediment Particles of sand, silt and clay that are carried by water and settle in a pond, river, lake or sea.

Slurry Water or liquid that is full of suspended particles.

Smog A visible haze that forms over a city due to vehicle air pollution.

Sustainable Resources or energy sources which can be maintained at a steady rate for future generations.

Trillion A million million.

Turbine A bladed wheel, turned by moving water or steam, which turns a generator to produce electricity.

Books to read

Science at the Edge: Alternative Energy Supplies Sally Morgan; Heinemann Library, 2002: a thorough look at renewable energy supplies.

Science at the Edge: Global Warming Sally Morgan; Heinemann Library, 2002; discusses how global warming is affecting our planet.

Sustainable Futures: Energy John Stringer; Evans Brothers 2005; looks at how energy will need to be used if we are to develop a sustainable future.

Websites

www.energy.gov/energysources/fossilfuels.htm The website of the US Department of Energy. It looks at fossil fuels and all the alternative energy sources, including solar and nuclear power.

www.energyquest.ca.gov A website developed by the California Energy Commission looking at all aspects of energy with information on solar power, alternative fuel vehicles and ways to save electricity.

www.scienceonline.co.uk/energy/nonrenewable.html These webpages look at non-renewable energy sources.

www.eia.doe.gov/kids/energyfacts/ This information-packed website has loads of information on both renewable and non-renewable energy sources, from coal and oil to wind and solar power.

www.foe.co.uk The website of Friends of the Earth. This organisation produces information on energy alternatives. It also has an education arm producing materials for teachers and young people.

Note: Page numbers in *italic* refer to illustrations.

ENERGY DEBATE

Contents of all titles in the series: